BEHIND THE SCENES BIOGRAPHIES

WHAT YOU NEVER KNEW ABOUT

>> ———————— <<

HARRY
STYLES

by Dolores Andral

CAPSTONE PRESS
a capstone imprint

Spark is published by Capstone Press, an imprint of Capstone
1710 Roe Crest Drive, North Mankato, Minnesota 56003
capstonepub.com

Library of Congress Cataloging-in-Publication Data
Names: Andral, Dolores, author.
Title: What you never knew about Harry Styles / Dolores Andral.
Description: North Mankato, Minnesota : Capstone Press, 2023. | Series: Behind the
scenes biographies | Includes bibliographical references and index. | Audience:
Ages 9-11 | Audience: Grades 4-6 | Summary: "Why did Harry Styles eat a water
scorpion? What does he do when he can't sleep? Readers will find out these answers
and more of everything they're dying to know about Harry Styles. High-interest
details and bold photos of his fascinating life will enthrall reluctant and struggling
readers, while carefully leveled text will leave them feeling confident"— Provided by
publisher.
Identifiers: LCCN 2022024624 (print) | LCCN 2022024625 (ebook) | ISBN
9781669003038 (hardcover) | ISBN 9781669040576 (paperback) | ISBN 9781669002994
(pdf) | ISBN 9781669003014 (kindle edition)
Subjects: LCSH: Styles, Harry, 1994—Juvenile literature. | Singers—England—
Biography—Juvenile literature. | LCGFT: Biographies.
Classification: LCC ML3930.S89 A53 2023 (print) | LCC ML3930.S89 (ebook) | DDC
782.42166092 [B]—dc23
LC record available at https://lccn.loc.gov/2022024624
LC ebook record available at https://lccn.loc.gov/2022024625

Editorial Credits
Editor: Erika L. Shores; Designer: Heidi Thompson; Media Researcher: Jo Miller;
Production Specialist: Tori Abraham

Image Credits
Getty Images: Anthony Pham, 25, Gareth Cattermole, Cover, Kevin Mazur, 7, 13,
15, 18, Mike Coppola, 29, Stuart C. Wilson, 27, Theo Wargo, 10; Shutterstock: Anant
Kasetsinsombut, 17 (bottom), Art Konovalov, 21 (top), dean bertoncelj, 19, Debby
Wong, 4, Executioner, 28, FlashStudio, 9, lev radin, 22, Mega Pixel, 24, Renatas
Repcinskas, 21 (bottom), sil_sil_sil, 16, Skylines, 14, Sunny_bu, 11, Yuangeng Zhang, 8

◇ ◇

TABLE OF CONTENTS

Words in **bold** are in the glossary.

BRING THE
STYLE!

Harry Styles can sing. He can act.
And he can *dress*! Harry says fashion
should be fun. Many people agree that
Harry's style is the best in the business.

FACT

Harry was on the cover of *Vogue* magazine.
He was the first man to be on it by himself.

CALLING ALL
STYLERS!

How much do you know about Harry?

Take this quiz to find out!

1. Why did Harry cut off his long hair?

2. What hit song started out as a joke? (Hint: Kids star in the video!)

3. What are Harry's favorite colors?

4. Where's one of the weirdest places Harry has seen his face?

5. What kind of music did Harry's first band, White Eskimo, play?

1. To star in the movie *Dunkirk* **2.** "Kiwi"

3. Orange and blue **4.** On pants **5.** Pop-punk

× × × × × × × × × × × × × × × × × ×
× × × × × × × × × × × × × × × ×

Harry once ate a giant water scorpion during a TV show. Why? He didn't want to answer a question about his One Direction bandmates. The question: Who does Harry think made the best album since leaving the group. We'll never know!

× × × × × × × × × × × ×

Members of One Direction

A HARRY
HALLOWEEN

Harry doesn't like dressing up for Halloween. But in 2021, two of his concerts fell on Halloween weekend. And guess what? Harry threw a giant party he called Harryween.

On October 30, Harry dressed up as Dorothy from *The Wizard of Oz*. The next day was Halloween. Harry wore a ruffled, white clown costume. He even had pearls on his face. Both nights he sported rings and bright nail polish.

FACT

Harry has a beauty brand called Pleasing. One of the first products was nail polish.

LET'S GO TO THE MOVIES

Harry's first movie role was in the movie *Dunkirk*. He gave up music for five months to work on the film. The director told him not to take acting lessons. He wanted Harry's role to feel **authentic**.

15

Would you like to visit a magical island? The music video for the song "Adore You" was set on one. It was called Eroda. The hashtag #VisitEroda went **viral**. But the island isn't real. Some fans figured out the name Eroda is *adore* spelled backward.

MY FAVORITE
THINGS

Harry has at least 50 tattoos. One was because of a bet! If the Green Bay Packers football team won a certain game, he would get a tattoo of the team logo. Harry was sure they would win. He got the tattoo before the game was played. The Packers lost. Good thing it's his favorite football team!

What does Harry do when he can't sleep? He goes out for a drive. He says it's relaxing. Can you name the awesome cars he's been spotted in? Try a Ferrari, a Jaguar, and an Audi!

FACT

What else does Harry do when he can't sleep? He meditates. It calms his mind and body.

TREAT PEOPLE WITH KINDNESS

Harry fed a fan's goldfish when she wasn't home. He gave leftover food to a **paparazzi**. He bought pizzas for people without homes. Harry even donated his long hair to a **charity**. The group makes wigs for people with cancer.

"I think it's just a time right now where we could use a little more kindness and empathy and patience with people ..."

—Harry Styles (*Vogue*, November 13, 2020)

Fans flock to Harry's concerts. Many shows sell out. In 2021, Harry's tour raised more than $1 million for charities. One group gives food to families. Another charity helps clean up the environment. Another one helps doctors.

FAMILY FASHION

Harry has a sister named Gemma. She is three years older than him. She doesn't like to dress up like Harry. But she joined him on a magazine **fashion shoot**. They wanted to surprise their mom with it.

Gemma

Where does Harry keep the outfits he's worn at his concerts? He has a secret **vault**. It's in London. Cameras record it 24 hours a day. The clothes are frozen. This **preserves** them. Now that's cool!

Glossary

authentic (ah-THEN-tik)—real, genuine, or true

charity (CHAYR-uh-tee)—a group that raises money or collects goods to help people in need

fashion shoot (FASH-uhn SHOOT)—an event where people wearing fashionable clothes get their photographs taken

paparazzi (pah-puh-RAHT-see)—a photographer who takes pictures of celebrities, or a reporter who writes about them in an unfriendly way

preserve (pri-ZURV)—to protect something so it stays in its original state

vault (VAWLT)—a room or compartment used to keep something safe

viral (VYE-rul)—quickly and widely spread through social media

Read More

Bach, Greg. *Harry Styles*. Broomall, PA: Mason Crest, 2023.

Barghoorn, Linda. *Harry Styles*. New York: Crabtree Publishing Company, 2018.

Schwartz, Heather E. *Harry Styles: Pop Star with an X Factor*. Minneapolis: Lerner Publications, 2022.

Internet Sites

50 Fun Facts About Harry Styles
thefactsite.com/50-harry-styles-facts/

Harry Styles Official Website
hstyles.co.uk/

Harry Styles: Style Evolution
vogue.co.uk/gallery/harry-styles-style-evolution

Index

About the Author

Dolores Andral earned an MFA from Queens University in Charlotte, NC. She loves writing for kids because she believes children should see themselves reflected in the books they read. She lives with her husband and four kids in Washington State.